ART OF WAR, VERSION 2.0

Sun Tzu for the Twenty-First Century

By Keith Bendis and Joe Queenan

FANTAGRAPHICS UNDERGROUND

SEATTLE, WASHINGTON

For Betzie, as always. —KB

To Francesca. —JQ

The Art of War was written 2,500 years ago, either by a brilliant strategist named Sun Tzu or by a group of brilliant strategists who pooled their wisdom and published it under Sun Tzu's name for reasons they never officially divulged. This is not as unusual as it seems. Just as *The Iliad* was probably not written by a man named Homer but by a whole phalanx of Greek poets, and just as Robert Ludlum's recent books were almost certainly not written by Robert Ludlum, who has been dead for 21 years, the true authorship of *Art of War* is shrouded in mystery.

From the marketing perspective, shrouding the true authorship of a book in mystery is a cunning tactic. In the West, where the book has long been obligatory reading for military leaders, putting out a book called *The Art of War by Sun Tzu* is a whole lot more attention-grabbing than publishing *The Art of War by Fred Schwarz*. Or *The Art of War By a Bunch of Brilliant Strategists*. For practical purposes, in this version of the book we will refer to Sun Tzu as the sole author of *The Art of War*, even if this is not true. Otherwise things get too confusing.

For the record, *The Art of War* is not called *The Art of War* in China. It is called *Sun Tzu*.

The original edition of *The Art of War* was not profusely illustrated with witty and amusing drawings. This is probably because people in the ancient world did not have much of a sense of humor. At the very least, they did not like mixing humor with serious material about warfare. The version you are holding in your hands, with clever, tongue-in-cheek drawings by Keith Bendis, confirms the eternal truth that there is almost nothing in life that is not worth chuckling about. It's just that it sometimes takes people 2,500 years to get around to it.

The basic premise of *The Art of War* is that the greatest victories are achieved by those who never need to shed blood, those who can achieve their ends through the delicate arts of diplomacy. This is a noble sentiment. A noble, noble sentiment. But once Sun Tzu gets that noble sentiment out of the way he spends the next 13 chapters explaining how to kill off your enemies.

This is one of the central paradoxes about the book. If Sun Tzu's main objective is to teach people how to avoid bloodshed, why then has his book been enthusiastically read by everyone from Douglas Macarthur to Mao Zedong to Norman Schwarzkopf, all of whom made their living by killing people? There is certainly no record that the book was ever read by St. Francis of Assisi or Florence Nightingale or Mother Teresa or Mahatma Gandhi. In short, no matter what anyone tries to tell you, *The Art of War* is a how-to guide to making war.

Sun Tzu usually speaks in short, terse sentences that are easy to remember. This is why the book has long been popular among America's CEOs, because suits hate complexity. Among his most useful suggestions are the following:

"To know your enemy, you must become your enemy."

"You have to believe in yourself."

"Attack like the fire and be still as the mountain."

"Keep your friends close and your enemies closer."

Not everything that Sun Tzu says is worth committing to memory. It is no insult to the author to point out that a lot of the book is filler. In Sun Tzu's defense, this is equally true of famous how-to guides like Machiavelli's *The Prince* and Henry David Thoreau's *Walden*. You could say the same thing about the Bible, which is loaded with extraneous material of little use to anyone. What, after all, is the point of *The Book of Numbers*? And why do we need not one, not two, but four evangelists — Matthew, Mark, Luke and John — to tell us the exact same story? The answer to this question is also shrouded in mystery. Bear in mind that *The Art of War* is a tiny, tiny, tiny book, and if it only contained the 25 or 30 incontestably incisive pearls of wisdom the author offered up, it wouldn't constitute much more than an ancient Chinese Power Point presentation or a flimsy pamphlet. Pamphlets are rarely taken seriously, whereas books are. But in order to pad out his *opus magnum* to book length, Sun Tzu had to fill *The Art of War* with a large number of boilerplate assertions that would be obvious to even the dullest child.

Here are a few examples:

"The art of war is of vital importance to the state. It is a matter of life and death, a road either to safety or to ruin. Hence, it is a subject of inquiry that under no circumstances can be neglected."

Correct.

"Now, in order to kill the enemy, our men must be roused to anger."

Also correct.

"Even the finest sword plunged into salt water will eventually rust."

No argument here.

The Art of War abounds with innumerable incontestable truths of this nature, but this does not mean that Sun Tzu can be accused of phoning it in. In many cases, he says unbelievably obvious things just to keep readers on their toes, to see if they're paying attention. Like a high school teacher abruptly halting his lesson to ask: "You there, McGregor, what is the capital of the United States?" Sun Tzu wants to make sure that the reader is not nodding off in the middle of class.

It is also worth remembering that, just as armies have good days and bad days, even the greatest military tacticians occasionally wake up and realize: "Oh boy, today I got nothing." This explains insipid filler material like:

"When, in consequence of heavy rains up-country, a river which you wish to ford is swollen, and flecked with foam, wait until it subsides."

Yes. Definitely wait.

"If the enemy leaves a door open, you must rush in."

Yes, you must.

"Be where your enemy is not."

Yes. Be there. For if your enemy can't find you, he can't kill you. There is one other possible explanation for the enormous number of head-scratchingly obvious statements in *The Art of War*. The book was written 2,500 years ago. A lot of things have changed since then, particularly with the development of modern weapons. It is entirely possible that 2,501 years ago, just before Sun Tzu wrote *The Art of War*, military strategists did not know that if the enemy leaves the door open, you must rush in. Now, thanks to him, they did.

   The Art of War has stood the test of time in part because it is cogent, wise and comprehensive, but also because Sun Tzu got there first. Later military strategists like Julius Caesar and William the Conqueror and Saladin and Cochise could effortlessly have deduced that warfare is too important an activity for a leader to overlook and that when confronted with much larger forces, the best policy is to run away. In fact, there may even have been strategists who preceded Sun Tzu and knew all these things, but they never got around to writing them down. Sun Tzu did. That is why his fame lives on, while the renown of so many others have been forgotten. In the words of one sage: For best results, get there firstest with the mostest.

Chapter I — Laying Plans
All warfare is based on deception.

Laying Plans for Warfare is Based on Deception

SUN TZU WROTE *THE ART OF WAR* 800 years after the end of the Trojan War. As is well known, it took the Greeks 10 long years to triumph over the Trojans because they wasted all their time and energy laying siege to a walled city where the besieged had plenty of food and ammunition stored away. Thousands died needlessly because of the stubborn, dimwit Spartan and Mycenean generals. Nor were Achilles and his flighty Myrmidons much help. Not until the invaders tricked the defenders into bringing a stupid wooden horse filled with Greek soldiers into the previously impregnable city did mighty Troy finally fall. Proving that the Trojans were even dumber than the Greeks. Which was going some.

The lesson Sun Tzu derived from this seminal event is obvious: Never waste your time besieging a walled city whose defenders can effortlessly lounge around the parapets pouring vats of boiling hot pitch onto your hapless troops without incurring many casualties of their own. Instead, go immediately to the time-honored ruse of stuffing a wooden horse filled with warriors who will sneak out of the structure at night and open the city gates so that your soldiers can rush in and put everyone to the sword. As Sun Tzu once confided to a group of warlike but hopelessly unsophisticated Chinese generals: "When it's a choice between a costly 10-year siege and resorting to a dumb-assed trick, swallow your pride and build the goddamn horse. By the way, I really shouldn't have to tell you guys this stuff."

Chapter I - Laying Plans

The general who wins a battle makes many calculations before the battle is fought -

Chapter II - On Waging War

In chariot fighting when ten or more chariots have been taken those should be rewarded who took the first. Our own flags should be substituted for those of the enemy. The captured soldiers should be kindly treated and kept This is called using the conquered fo to augment one's own strength

Waging War

SUN TZU'S ADHERENTS INSIST that his ideas are as relevant today as they were 2,500 years ago, but this is not true. Many of Sun Tzu's suggestions are only applicable to warfare in ancient societies. For example, in olden days, it was possible to seize the enemy's chariots, remodel them ever so slightly, change the insignias and add them to one's own fleet. This process is often referred to as "Diversionary Decaling."

Unfortunately in modern warfare, this tactic will no longer work. Different countries use different styles of tanks and even if you stuck an American flag on a Russian tank, American soldiers would keep firing away at it because they would know that Russians were inside. Chinese tanks don't look like French tanks, nor do Bolivian tanks look like Jamaican tanks, so the same general rule applies.

This is one of the many areas where Sun Tzu's advice is no longer useful, because war was simpler back in his era. It is a little-known fact that back in days of yore, everybody basically bought their chariots from the same chariot maker: Hephaestus of Ithaca & Sons. So, if the Trojans seized a bunch of Greek chariots and then covered them with their own flags, nobody on the battlefield would get confused because all ancient chariots looked pretty much alike. The Trojans might have chariots that looked like Fords while the Greeks had chariots that looked like Chevys. But nobody had chariots that looked like Humvees.

Things did not get confusing until armies started turning up with fancy, highly detailed chariots adorned with gaudy images of hydras and centaurs and minotaurs and unicorns. We are speaking here of the Assyrians, the Medes, and of course the Hittites, who always let things get a little bit out of control. Hittite chariots could not be seized and repurposed as Egyptian chariots because they were far too ornate and could be spotted a mile away. It is not Sun Tzu's fault that he did not anticipate this revolution in warcraft design. But it indicates once again that not everything Sun Tzu says can be applied to modern warfare.

Chapter III - Attack by Stratagem

The worst policy of all is to besiege walled cities.
The general, unable to control his irritation, will
launch his men to the assault like swarming ants
with the result that one third of his men are slain, while
the town still remains untaken—

The Sheathed Sword

SUN TZU DOES NOT LIKE EMPERORS or kings or royalty in general, feeling that warfare should be left to the professionals. Whenever royalty gets involved, as has been shown time and time again throughout history, they needlessly confuse the issue by first telling their troops to do this and then to do that. For every mighty warrior king like Henry v or Charlemagne, seasoned veterans who really knew their way around a battlefield, there is a Xerxes or an Edward ii or a Bonnie Prince Charlie, who make a mess of the whole operation with their ridiculous clothes and silly nicknames and inane suggestions.

Sun Tzu also believes that in waging war image is everything. In his opinion, it is impossible to wage war while being ferried around in a glitzy sedan chair, because sedan chairs powered by four to six humans can't move as quickly as chariots or horses and are completely useless during retreats, especially headlong routs. Also, the sight of a preening potentate lounging in a fancy sedan chair demoralizes the working-class troops because it suggests that the emperor, tsar, khan or king thinks that waging war is some kind of joke. War, as Sun Tzu reminds us again, is not for amateurs. And it is certainly not for clowns.

Chapter III – The Sheathed Sword

One way a sovereign can bring misfortune upon his army:
By commanding the army to advance or retreat, being ignorant
of the fact that it cannot obey. This is called hobbling the army.

Chapter IV - Tactics

To secure ourselves against defeat lies in our own hands, but the opportunity of defeating the enemy is provided by the enemy himself. Hence the saying: One may know how to conquer without being able to do it.

Tactics

SUN TZU SAYS that it possible for an army to make itself invincible, but this does not necessarily mean that an invincible army will vanquish every enemy. It only means that an invincible army will not be conquered itself. For example, if an invincible army fights a vincible army, it will win. But if an invincible army faces off against another invincible army, the battle will end in a tie.

And if an army gets too big for its boots and erroneously convinces itself that it is invincible and then attacks an authentically invincible enemy, it will find out the hard way that it is not invincible. This is what happens every time a foreign army invades Afghanistan. Thought you were invincible, Persians, Mongols, English, Russians, Americans? Think again.

How can you tell if your army is truly invincible? Well, you can get a pretty clear reading on the invincibility issue if you head due east and attack Russia, the way Napoleon Bonaparte did in 1812 and Adolf Hitler did in 1941. If you get your ass whipped the way the French and the Germans did in those two disastrous incursions, it means that you were in fact a vincible army while the Russians were invincible. In short, you got just a bit too cocky, like the Baltimore Colts did when they played the New York Jets in Super Bowl III. In warfare, as in boxing, you're only invincible until proven otherwise. And that's it.

For best results, if you think that you are invincible but are not 100%

sure, take your army out for a dry run and invade Italy or Belgium or Greece or Ethiopia first. In a pinch, Norway or Scotland will do. If you immediately get bogged down, or victory comes at too high a price, it means that you were not as invincible as you thought you were. A case in point: Until the Battle of the Little Big Horn, George Armstrong Custer was absolutely, 100% sure that the mighty Seventh Cavalry was invincible.

Boy, was *he* ever wrong!

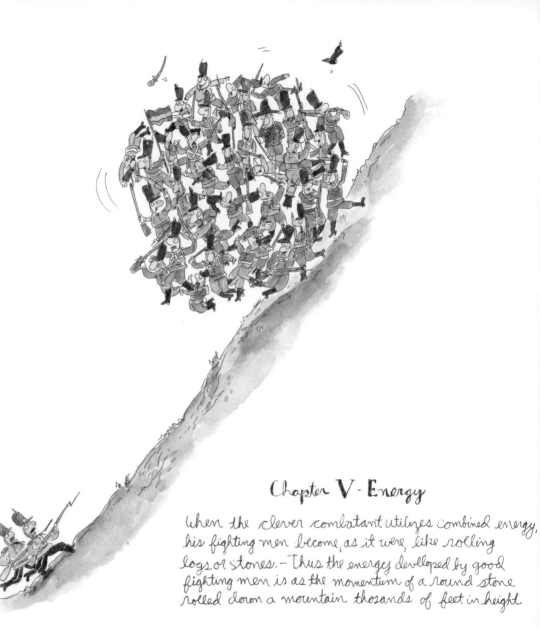

Chapter V - Energy

When the clever combatant utilizes combined energy, his fighting men become, as it were, like rolling logs or stones. — Thus the energy developed by good fighting men is as the momentum of a round stone rolled down a mountain thousands of feet in height.

Energy

SUN TZU IS A GREAT BELIEVER in momentum and enthusiasm. So, if you can really get your troops pumped up before a battle, you will almost certainly prevail.

But Sun Tzu is also a great believer in attacking an enemy from above. The reason is, if you order your troops to run downhill at the enemy, some of them will trip and thereby trip the soldiers behind them who will then trip the soldiers behind them, and so on and so forth until the attackers finally resemble a gigantic ball rolling down a hill. At this point, it doesn't matter if your troops are still upright: The impact of their centrifugal force will bowl over the enemy like a bunch of ten pins. Then your troops can pull themselves up off the ground and bayonet or disembowel the enemy forces, now flying flat on the ground.

This tactic will not work if you try to roll your army upward.

Chapter VI - Weak Points and Strong

Whoever is first in the field and awaits the coming
of the enemy will be fresh for the fight; whoever is second
in the field and has to hasten to battle will arrive exhausted.

Weak Points and Strong Points

SUN TZU SAYS that an army should arrive on the battlefield before the enemy does, so that by the time the enemy shows up he will be completely exhausted. This was definitely true 2,500 years ago because armies mostly traveled on foot. In the modern world, with helicopters and jeeps and armored personnel carriers, both armies can arrive at the battle site tan and rested, fresh as a daisy, with no lingering after-effects from travel. So in this case it really doesn't matter who shows up first.

But in this chapter, Sun Tzu is trying to make a broader point. The army that shows up first probably wants to fight more than the Johnny-Come-Latelies. That's why they marched 20 miles a day to get there. Or took an early flight. If you really, really wanted to get down and dirty with your enemy, you wouldn't spend days or weeks lollygagging in the desert or the mountains or the Hindu Kush or dallying in the flesh pots of Gomorrah or, even worse, the charnel houses of Babylon.

As Alexander the Great demonstrated again and again in his campaigns against the Thracians, the Corinthians, the Spartans and the Persians, the army that shows up first is obviously spoiling for a fight, chomping at the bit, ready to rock 'n roll, while the tardy, indecisive army that shows up second would really rather be elsewhere, and thus is cruising for a bruising. As children have been told by their mothers since time immemorial, punctuality counts.

Chapter VII - Maneuvering

We shall be unable to turn natural advantage
to account unless we make use of local guides.

Maneuvering

IN SUN TZU'S TIME, when an army invaded another country, it could not rely upon local road signs or mileage markers because the defenders would have repainted them to make the invaders think that east was west, that here was there, that up was down. The only way around this was to bribe or threaten a local guide to show the invaders how to get where they were going.

Xerxes, the arrogant king of the Persians, did not know this when he invaded Greece in 480 BC with an army so vast its numbers seemed to stretch forever. For days and days, his massive army tried to dislodge 300 plucky Spartans who had taken up their position inside a narrow mountain pass at Thermopylae. No luck.

At some point, one of Xerxes's adjutants must have come to him with a new, recently translated edition of *The Art of War.*

"You might want to take a look at Chapter VII," he would have said. "Pay particular attention to the part about using local guides to defeat the enemy."

Immediately after that, Xerxes's aides found a duplicitous goat-herd who had a bone to pick with the Spartans. The man was only too willing to show the Persians a secret path through the mountains, enabling them to surround the 300 Spartans and massacre them. Xerxes then marched on Athens and destroyed it. Without Sun Tzu's advice, Xerxes's army might still be stalled outside that legendary mountain pass. So take the lesson to heart: When invading a foreign company with challenging terrain, try finding yourself a treasonous local goatherd.

They're usually not all that hard to find.

Chapter VIII - Variation of Tactics

There are five dangerous faults that may affect a general, of which the first two are recklessness, which leads to destruction; and cowardice, which leads to capture.

Variation in Tactics

IN THIS CHAPTER, Sun Tzu lays out "The Nine Transformations," which are distinct methods of employing one's forces. He specifically says:

1 In difficult country, do not pitch camp.
2 In country where high roads intersect, join hands with your allies.
3 Do not linger in dangerously isolated positions.
4 In hemmed-in ground, you must resort to stratagem.
5 In desperate positions, you must fight.

Then he says:

1 There are roads which must not be followed.
2 There are armies which must not be attacked.
3 There are towns that must not be besieged.
4 There are positions that must not be contested.
5 There are commands of the sovereign that must not be obeyed.

Hang on a second. Unless I'm very much mistaken, five and five makes…well, you do the math. It shows no disrespect to Sun Tzu to point out that his list contains 10 transformations and not 9. Why didn't anyone spot this error over the last 2,500 years? Simple. Editors did not exist in the time of Sun Tzu, nor did professional proofreaders. Back in those days they only had scribes and calligraphers. Fact-checkers did not come into existence until the Renaissance.

Second, once a book has been in print for 2,500 years, modern editors are reluctant to tamper with the text, because this would force them to do one of the following:

1. Rename "The 9 Transformations" as "The 10 Transformations."
2. Cut out one of the Transformations entirely.
3. Admit that Sun Tzu was weak on math.

But this would be like pointing out that Shakespeare gets his history all wrong in *Julius Caesar* or that nobody named Macbeth ever actually lived in Cawdor Castle.

No fussy-pants editor or translator, scraping by on a pittance in a modern publishing house, is willing to take on a titan like Sun Tzu.

So "The 9 transformations" it is.

Chapter IX - The Army On The March

When an invading force crosses a river in its onward march, do not advance to meet it in midstream. It will be best to let half the army get across and then deliver your attack.

The Army on the March

SUN TZU IS AT HIS MOST PRESCIENT when he advises a defending army to wait until the enemy is hallway across a river before attacking. This is especially true of the Nile, which is full of voracious crocodiles and dyspeptic hippos, and of the Amazon, which is teeming with man-eating piranhas. In Sun Tzu's considered opinion, why risk suffering needless casualties when you can get fierce anacondas and famished sea serpents to do the heavy lifting? Think it through, guys.

Sun Tzu's dictum does not apply to all bodies of water. If the enemy is fording a stream, rivulet, brook or pond, pounce. Same deal for creeks, marshes, estuaries and fjords. With bays and inlets, proceed with caution.

And if the enemy is trying to attack across the English Channel — 22 miles across at its narrowest point — as the Spanish foolishly did in 1589, pull up a chair and wait for the notoriously inclement British weather to do the damage. Indeed, Sun Tzu is reputed to have once said: "When fighting an enemy who invades by sea, the wise general sticks to *terra firma*. The more firmer, the less terror."

Chapter X - Terrain

With regard to **precipitous heights**, if you precede your adversary, occupy the raised and sunny spots and there wait for him to come.

Terrain

AN AWFUL LOT of *The Art of War* is devoted to the importance of being able to fire *down* on the enemy. In this chapter, the ancient Chinese sage reminds readers once again that if you arrive at the foot of a hill, you should climb it immediately because then you will have your enemy at a huge disadvantage.

Pretty obvious, right? So one would think. But in fact, even though everyonewho is anyone in the world of military science claims to have read *The Art of War*, this is obviously not true. The French foolishly ceded the tropical heights to the Viet Minh in the disastrous battle of Dien Bien Phu in 1954, and when George Pickett led his catastrophic charge against the entrenched Union forces at the Battle of Gettysburg in 1863, his forces got massacred by the Yankees — who had occupied the higher ground since Day 1 of the battle. This strongly suggests that neither George Pickett nor Robert E. Lee had ever bothered to read *The Art of War*. Or if they did they didn't take notes.

Many military experts believe that if the Confederates had won the Battle of Gettysburg, they might have won the Civil War. However, many of these so-called experts are aggrieved Southerners, bitter and embarrassed by the fact that the South, always tough customers when fighting on their own turf, couldn't win on the road. So, let us repeat Sun Tzu's dictum one more time: If you see a hill, climb it. Unless the enemy has already climbed it. If the enemy has already climbed it, run away.

Rapidity is the essence of war. Take advantage of the enemy's unreadiness, make your way by unexpected routes, and attack unguarded spots.

The Nine Situations

SNEAKING UP ON THE ENEMY from behind is one of the devious tactics that has been put to good use by fierce warriors as varied as Genghis Khan and Hannibal. Genghis Khan came in the back way through the mountains of Central Asia when he invaded Persia in 1215 and no one saw him coming. Millions died as a result.

Similarly, Hannibal invaded Italy through narrow mountain passes in Switzerland back in 219 B.C. To the shock of the Romans, he even brought along a herd of elephants. Absolutely no one saw that one coming either.

Yet as a tactician and conqueror, Genghis Khan was successful where Hannibal was not. In the space of eight years, the Khan's Golden Horde thundered across the steppes of Central Asia, laying waste to everything in their path and advanced as far as the gates of Vienna before their progress was halted by the Khan's untimely death. Nevertheless, Genghis Khan could legitimately lay claim to having briefly presided over the greatest empire the world has ever known.

By contrast, Hannibal's triumphs were piddling. After a series of spectacular victories when he first turned up, Hannibal spent the next 15 years roaming around Italy, raiding and pillaging, but never succeeding in bringing Rome to its knees. Why? One reason was that the Romans refused to come out and fight. But an even bigger reason is Hannibal's inexplicable obsession with elephants. Yes, okay, elephants had a certain PR value because they were so big and scary, and no one's going to quibble about that. But they definitely slowed things down.

Chapter XI - The Nine Situations

For those who have to fight in the ratio of one to ten, there is nothing better than a narrow pass.

Genghis Khan, taking Sun Tzu's dictum about rapidity to heart, deliberately did not invade Persia with a herd of chubby elephants, but with an army consisting almost entirely of fast, sleek war ponies. Ponies aren't anyway near as scary as elephants, but they can cover a lot more distance in a short space of time. Also, they eat less. If Hannibal had stuck to the Sun Tzu formula and invaded Italy with an army mounted on fast ponies, he would have crushed the Romans in two weeks flat. When you want to wage war, you bring an army, not a circus.

Had Sun Tzu lived long enough to witness Hannibal's epic failure, he would have probably added an extra chapter to *The Art of War*, warning generals not to overdo things. "When an army has already surprised the enemy by sneaking up on him through Switzerland, it is not necessary to rub it in by gallivanting around on a bunch of gaudy war elephants," he would have written. "Nobody likes a showoff."

Chapter XI - The Nine Situations

At the critical moment, the leader of an army acts like one who has climbed up a height and then kicks away the ladder behind him.

One other thing: Chapter XI contains virtually the same information as Chapter VIII, only this time it's 9 Situations instead of 9 Transformations. Once again, it looks like Sun Tzu's editors were asleep at the wheel when he handed in the final draft of the original manuscript. Either that or they simply felt that Sun Tzu was running on empty and recycling his material, but didn't want to mention it out of fear that he would take his book to another publisher.

In Chapter XI, as in Chapter VIII, it becomes clear that Sun Tzu really likes the number nine, and will combine things in clusters of nine whether it makes sense or not. This had a profound effect on subsequent writers. Throughout history, particularly in the West, most lists of suggestions have been limited to seven, as in *The Seven Habits of Highly Effective People*, *The Seven Pillars of Wisdom*, *The Magnificent Seven*, and The Seven Deadly Sins. As one medieval scribe explained it to the author of what were originally The Nine Deadly Sins, "After Sin Number Seven — the sin of sloth — we felt that you were kind of pushing it. Pride, greed, wrath, envy, lust and gluttony? Sure, no problem. The public could follow you on those six. But sloth? Seriously? Sloth?"

Chapter XI is a clearcut case where Sun Tzu was having a slow day and decided to repackage some advice from an earlier chapter, figuring that nobody would notice. And even if they did, so what? Anyone can have an off day. As the great Roman poet Horace once said of Homer, after noticing that he had reintroduced a character in *The Iliad* who he'd killed off much earlier in the book: "Even the Master nodded." And in Chapter XI, it is obvious that Sun Tzu nods.

Chapter XII - Attack by Fire

There are five ways of attacking by fire. The first is to burn soldiers in their camp; the second is to burn stores; the third is to burn baggage trains; the fourth is to burn arsenals and magazines; the fifth is to hurl dropping fire among the enemy.

CHAPTER XII

Attack by Fire

IN THE NEXT-TO-LAST CHAPTER OF HIS BOOK, Sun Tzu finally gets around to discussing the use of fire as a means of subduing an enemy. Why the delay? Simple. The *Art of War* starts out by encouraging military strategists to achieve their objectives without shedding blood, to use diplomacy to prevail over an adversary. But since fire consumes all that lays in its path, it obviously has no use as a diplomatic weapon. By the time you get around to burning down the topless towers of Ilium, it's pretty obvious that the time for diplomacy has passed.

Since Sun Tzu would prefer that the enemy voluntarily surrender to the invader, he buries the stuff about fire way, way in the back of the book. If the first chapter in the book was entitled "Attack by Fire," nobody would even bother to read the other 12 chapters. They'd just get out the matches and kindling and get cracking. Sun Tzu recognizes that the magician always saves his best trick for last.

As always, Sun Tzu has very specific suggestions when resorting to fire as a weapon. First, he says, wait till the ground is dry so that the flames will spread more quickly. Second, if possible, wait until you've got the wind at your back before starting the conflagration. Third, and make sure everybody is on the same page here, always make sure that you are standing behind the fire when you set it. And for best results, bring along lots and lots of water in case the blaze gets out of hand. For example, if the wind shifts and the flames start engulfing you.

Sun Tzu does not believe that a general should burn the enemy's city to the ground, because then there will be nothing left in the city to expropriate or annex or demand ransom for. Fire should be used judiciously, but sparingly, more as a terrifying threat than as an all-out assault weapon.

Finally, although Sun Tzu never directly addresses this issue, armies down through the ages expect to be given permission to sack cities after they have conquered them, as a sort of reward for a job well done. Prominent examples are Rome in 410 and 476, and Constantinople in 1453. But if you have already burned the city to the ground, there will be nothing left to sack, nothing left to plunder. This warning is sometimes referred to as Sun Tzu's Booty Call.

Chapter XIII - The Use of Spies

- the disposition of the enemy are ascertainable through spies and spies alone -

The Use of Spies

SUN TZU BELIEVES that the only foolproof way to know what the enemy has up his sleeve is to use spies. Spies come in all shapes and sizes. They can be courageous patriots planted inside the enemy's army, or avaricious scum bribed to betray their country, or they can simply be rock-solid professionals who spy for a living. In certain situations, spies can even be turncoat peasants or the aforementioned duplicitous goatherds. Though goatherds generally do not make great spies because they have to spend so much time herding their goats.

As the illustration makes clear, spies can only succeed if they don't actually look like spies; to pull off a top-notch espionage operation, they have to look like all the other soldiers in the army. Otherwise, they would stand out like a sore thumb. This is why the expression "cloak-and-dagger" is so erroneous, if not ridiculous. If a spy was actually dressed in a cloak while brandishing a dagger, it would be a dead giveaway that he was not playing for the home team.

Perhaps the best illustration of this rule is the case of the famous Dutch double agent "Mata Hari," who spied for the Germans during the First World War. Unlike most spies, who try to keep a low profile, Mata Hari actually had a day job in Paris as an exotic dancer. Mata Hari's flamboyance was her undoing; having drawn too much attention to herself in her nightclub act, she was shot by a French firing squad in 1917. Had she only read *The Art of War*, she would have had the good sense to pass herself off as a milliner or a seamstress or a remedial reading expert, and might have lived to a ripe old age. Her failure to do so resulted in her death. Sun Tzu would not have been one bit surprised by her unseemly demise.

"If you want to be an effective spy and your real name is Margaretha Geertruida MacLeod," he would have counselled her, "stick with Margaretha Geertruida MacLeod and leave the Mata Hari business out of it. As Hannibal found out the hard way with his ridiculous herd of circus elephants, keep being a show-off and see what happens."

Editor: Gary Groth
Design: Justin Allan-Spencer
Associate Publisher: Eric Reynolds
Publisher: Gary Groth

F.U. Press is an imprint of Fantagraphics Books Inc.
7563 Lake City Way NE
Seattle, WA 98115
fantagraphics.com/fu

ISBN: 978-1-68396-752-1
LOC #: 2022944376

First printing: February 2023
Printed in China
FU060